SPOTLIGHT ON THE AMERICAN INDIANS OF CALIFORNIA

THE ESSELEN

MIRANDA RATHJEN

PowerKiDS press™

NEW YORK

979.4
Ra

Published in 2018 by The Rosen Publishing Group, Inc.
29 East 21st Street, New York, NY 10010

Editor: Elizabeth Krajnik
Book Design: Michael Flynn
Interior Layout: Tanya Dellaccio

Photo Credits: Cover, p. 21 Doug Steakley/Lonely Planet Images/Getty Images; p. 5 Tupungato/Shutterstock.com; p. 6 Songquan Deng/Shutterstock.com; p. 7 David Litman/Shutterstock.com; pp. 9, 19 MPI/Archive Photos/Getty Images; pp. 10, 14 Courtesy of the Library of Congress; p. 11 Marilyn Angel Wynn/Corbis Documentary/ Getty Images; p. 13 https://commons.wikimedia.org/wiki/File:Monterey_native_c_1791.jpg; p. 15 Marilyn Angel Wynn/Nativestock/Getty Images; p. 17 Grafissimo/E+/Getty Images; p. 23 https://commons.wikimedia.org/wiki/ File:Charles_III_of_Spain_high_resolution.jpg; p. 24 Universal History Archive/Universal Images Group/Getty Images; p. 25 Mariusz S. Jurgielewicz/Shutterstock.com; p. 27 Bobbi Onia/Underwood Archives/Archive Photos/Getty Images; p. 29 https://commons.wikimedia.org/wiki/File:Carleton_Watkins_(American_-_(Mission,_San_Carlos_del_ Carmelo))_-_WGoogle_Art_Project.jpg.

Library of Congress Cataloging-in-Publication Data

Names: Rathjen, Miranda, author.
Title: The Esselen / Miranda Rathjen.
Description: New York : PowerKids Press, [2018] | Series: Spotlight on the
  American Indians of California | Includes index.
Identifiers: LCCN 2017019059| ISBN 9781538324592 (pbk. book) | ISBN
  9781538324608 (6 pack) | ISBN 9781538324561 (library bound book)
Subjects: LCSH: Esselen Indians--Juvenile literature. | Big Sur
  (Calif.)--History--Juvenile literature. | Indians of North
  America--California--Juvenile literature.
Classification: LCC E99.E85 R38 2018 | DDC 979.4/00497--dc23
LC record available at https://lccn.loc.gov/2017019059

Manufactured in China

CPSIA Compliance Information: Batch #BW18PK For further information contact Rosen Publishing, New York, New York at 1-800-237-9932.

CONTENTS

CHAPTER ONE

WHO WERE THE ESSELEN?

Groups of American Indians have lived in what is now coastal California for about 8,000 years. One of these groups is known today as the Esselen. The Esselen lived in the mountainous region south of Monterey Bay, an area known for being beautiful but rather difficult to live in.

From the few clues left behind by this group of American Indians, **anthropologists** have determined that they spoke a different language than their neighbors, which included the Ohlones and the Salinans. However, these groups shared similar **customs** and traditions. The Esselen used natural resources to survive in their harsh surroundings. They created ornamental objects and basic, but useful, tools. The groups living in this area ate similar foods and built similar homes.

While it isn't possible to find individual members of the Esselen today, this group's **legacy** lives on in the lives of its **descendants**.

The Esselen lived in the area near what is now Garrapata State Park, south of Monterey, California.

CHAPTER TWO

ESSELEN ENVIRONMENT

The Esselen lived throughout a large part of central California. This area was about 580 square miles (1,502 sq km) and stretched from Point Lopez to Big Sur and inward from the coast to the Upper Carmel Valley and Junípero Serra Peak.

BIG SUR

Big Sur is a stretch of California's coast bordered to the east by the Santa Lucia Mountains, which are known for having thick forests.

CARMEL VALLEY

The dynamic landscape of Esselen country is beautiful, but surviving here became difficult for the Esselen.

Scholars are unable to determine just when the Esselen and their **ancestors** came to this area or how large the Esselen population was. It's estimated that there were between 500 and 1,000 Esselen at any one time based on the population sizes of similar American Indian groups nearby.

The region in which the Esselen lived often had cold rain and frost. To shelter themselves from the harsh weather, the Esselen built a type of circular home called an *iwano*. An opening in the center of the roof of each *iwano* let smoke out and was covered with an animal hide when it rained.

CHAPTER THREE

HOMES AND VILLAGES

Scholars are unsure how many Esselen communities existed or where they were located. Natural resources in this area of central California were scarce, so it's likely that the largest Esselen communities had fewer than 200 members. Like other groups in the area, the Esselen likely settled near flowing water.

Each *iwano* was made from poles, bark, grass, and other organic materials. One or two related families may have lived in a single *iwano*, which could be 6 to 20 feet (1.8 to 6.1 m) wide. Esselen slept on reed mats or blankets.

Each *iwano* had a fire pit that was used to heat the home and make meals. However, when the weather was nice, the Esselen likely made the majority of their meals outside.

Research shows that the Esselen may have buried their dead in community cemeteries located near their villages.

Esselen *iwano* may have looked similar to the wigwams built by the Winnebago, who lived in present-day Wisconsin.

CHAPTER FOUR

WHAT DID THE ESSELEN EAT?

Although Esselen country could be difficult to live in, there was plenty of food to go around. The landscape offered a wide variety of resources, including berries, nuts, vegetables, and wild game such as rabbits and deer.

The Esselen also harvested plants and fished in the Pacific Ocean. Coastal communities of the Esselen

LANDSCAPE NEAR BIG SUR

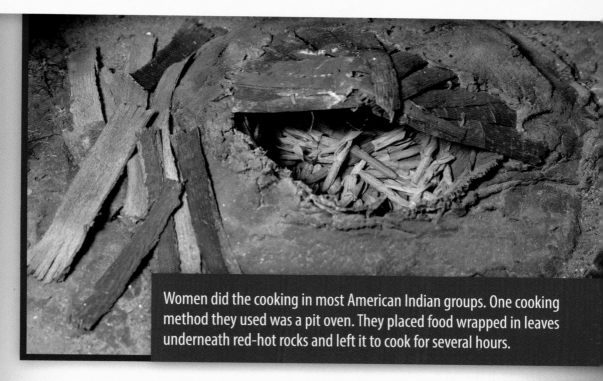

Women did the cooking in most American Indian groups. One cooking method they used was a pit oven. They placed food wrapped in leaves underneath red-hot rocks and left it to cook for several hours.

were especially fond of shellfish. Researchers have found big piles of shells in middens, or piles of trash, near what they believe were the sites of Esselen camps and villages.

The cooking methods used by the Esselen were likely similar to those of other American Indian groups in the area. Acorns were ground into powder and soaked in water to remove poisons. The Esselen likely cooked over an open flame or prepared food using steam or smoking methods. However, some foods could be eaten without preparation.

CHAPTER FIVE

ESSELEN FASHION

Central California's climate allowed American Indian groups to wear a wide variety of clothing. Some groups wore very little clothing to stay cool. The Esselen, however, probably wore different types of clothing than some of their neighbors.

Experts know very little about how the Esselen dressed, but they likely wore more clothing than other groups of American Indians due to the rain and cold temperatures in their region. When it was warm, Esselen men and young children probably wore little clothing, much like the members of other groups. The women living in this area wore two-piece skirts.

When the temperatures dropped and rain moved in, the Esselen likely used blankets, robes, and capes to cover up and stay warm. These coverings would have been made from animal fur and hides.

The Esselen may have dressed similar to the American Indians pictured here.

CREATIVITY AND USEFULNESS

Few Esselen **artifacts** have been found. Those that have suggest that members of this group of American Indians were highly skilled artists and craftspeople. Experts think that the Esselen produced artwork and crafts similar to those of their neighbors, the Ohlones and the Salinans.

The Esselen likely made good use of the animals they hunted. Clothing, blankets, and quivers for arrows could

The Esselen had many uses for plants and wood. They wove grasses and reeds to make baskets. Wood was used to make bows, arrows, and other tools. Some plants were used as medicines or poisons.

The Esselen ground acorns using mortars and pestles. They likely used the acorn powder as a type of flour.

be made from skins. Bones were transformed into beads, earrings, fishhooks, musical instruments, and tools. The Esselen likely decorated arrows, bows, capes, and dance skirts with feathers. Seashells from the area were used to make bowls, fishhooks, **razors**, and jewelry.

Stone was one of the most important resources for the Esselen. They used it to make mortars and pestles, which they used to grind things such as nuts and seeds. Stone was also used to make arrowheads and cutting tools.

CHAPTER SEVEN

LANGUAGE AND COMMUNITY

Since there are no remaining groups of Esselen today, understanding and learning about their culture and traditions is difficult. However, anthropologists do know the Esselen spoke a different language than their neighbors. This language was part of the larger Hokan language family. The Salinans and the Chumash spoke similar languages. Isabel Meadows was the last known person to **fluently** speak the Rumsen Ohlone language, which belonged to this language family. She died in 1939.

Scholars can only make guesses about how Esselen communities were structured. Some experts think the Esselen communities formed a political **alliance** called a tribelet. Others think there were five or six political groups who shared a common language and culture. These groups likely came together to form a single nation during times of conflict.

Most American Indian groups in California were probably led by chiefs. Village elders aided their chiefs. The position of chief was passed down from father to son.

CHAPTER EIGHT

ESSELEN WARFARE

The Esselen likely fought wars with their neighbors. The Ohlones were their main enemy. However, they got along well with the Salinans. The Esselen fought mainly with bows and arrows and spears, and they were known for their archery skills.

Most conflicts between groups of American Indians in California consisted of **raids**. Young warriors would invade enemy territory, capturing or killing anyone they found. Sometimes they destroyed whole villages. To end a war, the chiefs of the two groups would come to a peace agreement.

Sometimes the Esselen worked out conflict without full-blown warfare. They would meet at a certain place and time to perform a **ritual** war. The groups would perform dances, songs, and other rituals to show their bravery. One or two warriors would be killed, and then one side would surrender.

Wars started for a number of reasons. Sometimes groups fought over natural resources, such as hunting-and-gathering areas. The Esselen may have performed victory dances. This group of American Indians is pictured performing a "scalp dance" to celebrate victory over their enemies.

CHAPTER NINE

RELIGION AND FOLKLORE

In many American Indian groups from coastal and central California, both men and women could become spiritual leaders. These individuals were highly respected and often feared. They were said to have special abilities that could be used for both good and evil. They knew many songs, dances, and rituals, which the Esselen believed had the power to make people well or sick. They also believed spiritual leaders had the power to control the weather.

One way the Esselen may have expressed their religious beliefs was through rock art. Symbols marked on cave walls and rocks with paint are called pictographs. Pictures carved into a rock's surfaced are called petroglyphs.

Song and dance were other ways the Esselen expressed their religious beliefs. Like their neighbors, the Esselen probably played musical instruments such as flutes and whistles while they sang and danced.

This rock art may have been a way of celebrating a person's life or marking their death.

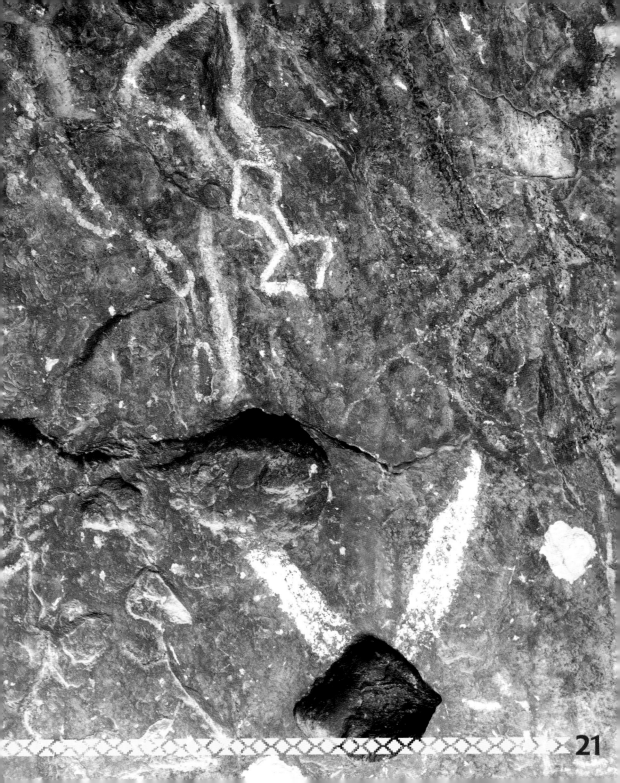

CHAPTER TEN

EUROPEAN ENCOUNTERS

Europeans began sailing along the California coast starting in the early 16th century. However, the first official landing didn't happen until Juan Rodríguez Cabrillo discovered San Diego Bay on September 28, 1542. Exploration of California continued and, in 1602, Sebastian Vizcaíno became the first European to explore the general region occupied by the Esselen.

Over the next 150 years or so, many more Europeans came to California. They brought diseases to which the native people had no immunity. These diseases killed many native people throughout North America, including those groups of American Indians living in California.

In the late 1700s, King Carlos III of Spain ordered **missions** to be built in California. He wanted to gain control of the area. He tried to do this by sending missionaries to develop friendships with the American Indian people of California and convert them to Spanish citizens.

King Carlos III of Spain was fearful that England and Russia would gain control of California and take over the Spanish territories in Mexico and Peru. He thought gaining the help of the American Indian people who lived in California would help him keep a strong hold on the Spanish empire.

CHAPTER ELEVEN

THE MISSION SAN CARLOS BORROMEO

Missions in California were more than just churches where native people were educated about Christianity. Each mission also educated native people about the Spanish way of life. The Mission San Carlos Borromeo is a Roman Catholic parish set up by the Spaniards. It was founded on June 3, 1770, in the Carmel Valley.

The first mission consisted of a small wooden fort that protected a church and a home for the priests and a few soldiers. Outside the fort were two villages in which the Esselen and Ohlones lived.

PRESENT-DAY MISSION CARMEL

The priests at the Mission San Carlos Borromeo promised the Esselen people friendship, help during times of war, and opportunities to gain access to steel, new kinds of food, and new livestock if they stayed and lived at the mission.

The Esselen were hesitant to move to the mission. The priests had formed friendships with the Esselen's enemies, the Ohlones. However, the Esselen moved to the mission anyway—perhaps to make sure the Ohlones didn't have an advantage over them.

CHAPTER TWELVE

TRANSITIONING TO THE EUROPEAN LIFESTYLE

From the late 18th century to the early 19th century, the Mission San Carlos Borromeo grew and seemed to succeed. A new mission was built in 1780 to better serve the American Indians and priests living there.

For the most part, the priests didn't try to change the natives' lives. However, the new followers—whom the priests called neophytes—began to adopt a more European lifestyle. Soon, the American Indians moved out of their traditional houses and into **adobe** homes. They performed Spanish music with their own **orchestras** and sang religious songs in Latin and the Ohlone and Esselen languages. They also began wearing some European-style clothing and using household tools that were just like the ones found among the Spanish colonists.

At the mission, the neophytes served as expert farmers and cowboys. Without their efforts, the mission wouldn't have been successful.

The missionaries taught some American Indian groups skills such as how to make adobe bricks like the ones pictured here.

CHAPTER THIRTEEN

THE ESSELEN DIE OUT

The diseases brought to North America by Europeans continued to threaten American Indian populations. Although the Mission San Carlos Borromeo succeeded in the early 19th century, the neophyte population decreased. More people died each year than were born. The priests did their best to help the sick, but some of their medicines and remedies ended up making the natives sicker.

Mission San Carlos Borromeo's future didn't look promising. As the population shrank, colonists from the nearby town of Monterey tried to occupy the best mission lands. In 1803, the new leader of the missions in California moved from San Carlos to the Chumash mission settlement at Santa Barbara.

In 1822, just after the end of the Mexican War of Independence, the Spanish army surrendered California to Mexico. The mission now belonged to Mexico. In 1834, the mission officially closed.

The U.S.-Mexican War (1846–1848) changed everything for the American Indians living in California. The treaty of 1848 made California a part of the United States. The U.S. government took away almost all of the American Indians' basic rights. After the mission closed, it fell into disrepair.

CHAPTER FOURTEEN

WHAT REMAINS?

Today, very little record of Esselen culture and history before the European arrival in California remains. During the early 20th century, anthropologists began to study the American Indian groups from California. By that time, people who spoke the Esselen language or identified themselves as Esselen could not be found.

Over time, many of the Esselen and their descendants married Ohlones. Today, there are no true Esselen left. However, over 600 members of tribes from the Monterey Bay region belong to the Ohlone Costanoan Esselen Nation. The nation is working toward becoming a federally recognized tribe.

Researchers have found some Esselen artifacts, which are now displayed at and cared for by a number of universities in California. The loss of the Esselen and their customs and language is a tragic part of American history. However, their legacy lives on in their descendants and their artifacts.

GLOSSARY

adobe (uh-DOH-bee) A kind of brick made from mud and straw.

alliance (uh-LY-unts) A close association formed between people or groups of people to reach a common objective.

ancestor (AN-ses-ter) Someone in your family who lived long before you.

anthropologist (an-thruh-PAH-luh-jist) A scientist who studies the history and society of humans.

artifact (AR-tuh-fakt) Something made by humans in the past that still exists.

custom (KUS-tum) An action or way of behaving that is traditional among the people in a certain group or place.

descendant (dih-SEN-dent) Someone related to a person or a group of people who lived at an earlier time.

fluently (FLOO-uhnt-lee) Easily and well.

legacy (LEH-guh-see) Something that comes from someone in the past.

mission (MIH-shun) A community established by a church for the purpose of spreading its faith.

orchestra (OR-kes-truh) A large group of people who play music together with many instruments.

raid (RAYD) A surprise attack by an enemy.

razor (RAY-zuhr) A sharp instrument used to shave hair from the face, body, or head.

ritual (RIH-choo-uhl) A religious ceremony, especially one consisting of a series of actions performed in a certain order.

INDEX

PRIMARY SOURCE LIST

Page 10
View of the coast from Highway 1 near Big Sur, California. Photograph. Created by Carol M. Highsmith. Between 1980 and 2006. Now kept at the Library of Congress Prints and Photographs Division Washington, D.C.

Page 14
Basketry of the Mission Indians. Photograph. Created by Edward S. Curtis. ca. 1924. Now kept at the Library of Congress Prints and Photographs Division Washington, D.C.

Page 23
Charles III. Painting. Created by Anton Raphael Mengs. ca. 1765. Now kept at the Museo del Prado Madrid, Spain.

WEBSITES

Due to the changing nature of Internet links, PowerKids Press has developed an online list of websites related to the subject of this book. This site is updated regularly. Please use this link to access the list: www.powerkidslinks.com/saic/essel